The Sovereignty Blueprint

Unlocking Wealth, Privacy, and Freedom with the Private Irrevocable, Exodus Trust and Vortex Banking

JOSH NELSON

MW01170390

copyright © 2024

Introduction

Breaking Free from the System

For centuries, individuals have been unknowingly integrated into systems designed to prioritize government and corporate interests. The tools of this control—taxes, regulations, and oversight—limit individual freedom and stifle innovation.

Despite the overwhelming power of these systems, a legal and ethical pathway exists to step outside their control. This book introduces two transformative tools: the Non-Grantor Irrevocable Private Complex Discretionary Spendthrift Trust (referred to as the Ecclesiastical Trust) and the Private Membership Association (PMA).

These structures are not loopholes or evasions of the law. Instead, they leverage legal principles and constitutional protections to reclaim the sovereignty that is every individual's birthright.

What You'll Learn in This Book

1. The history and legal foundation of ecclesiastical trusts.
2. How private law principles can help you build wealth and protect assets.
3. The role of PMAs in fostering privacy and community.

4. Real-world applications of these tools in achieving financial independence.

5. How to create generational wealth using life insurance within an ecclesiastical trust.

This book will guide you step by step, from understanding these structures to implementing them in your life.

Chapter 1
The Foundations of Ecclesiastical Law

Historical Context

Ecclesiastical law originates from religious institutions seeking to preserve their autonomy from government interference. From medieval Europe to modern-day America, churches have utilized trusts to hold property, manage resources, and maintain independence.

For example, early Christian churches in Europe created ecclesiastical trusts to protect their wealth during times of political upheaval. These trusts safeguarded assets from seizure by the state and provided financial stability for future generations.

Legal Protections

Constitutional Protections: The First Amendment guarantees the separation of church and state, ensuring that ecclesiastical trusts operate beyond the jurisdiction of secular authorities.

Jurisdictional Separation: Ecclesiastical trusts exist in the private domain, governed by religious principles rather than statutory laws. This allows for greater flexibility, privacy, and protection.

Case Law Precedent: Numerous court decisions affirm the autonomy of ecclesiastical entities, reinforcing their ability to operate independently.

Why Ecclesiastical Law is Relevant Today

Modern applications of ecclesiastical law extend beyond religious institutions. Families and individuals can establish trusts rooted in these principles to achieve financial sovereignty, asset protection, and privacy.

Chapter 2

Non-Grantor Irrevocable Private Complex Discretionary Spendthrift Trusts

What Makes These Trusts Unique?

1. Irrevocability: Once created, the terms of the trust cannot be altered, ensuring stability and long-term protection.

2. Spendthrift Provisions: Beneficiaries are protected from creditors and legal claims, ensuring the trust's assets remain secure.

3. Non-Grantor Status: The grantor relinquishes control of the trust assets, legally separating them from personal liabilities.

4. Complex Discretionary Nature: Trustees have full discretion over how assets are managed and distributed, providing flexibility to adapt to changing circumstances.

Benefits of an Ecclesiastical Trust

1. Privacy: The trust operates entirely in the private domain, shielded from public scrutiny.

2. Tax Advantages: Properly structured ecclesiastical trusts are immune to federal income taxes, capital gains taxes, and estate taxes.

3. Legal Immunity: Assets within the trust are protected from lawsuits, liens, and government claims.

Real-World Example: A Family Protecting Their Wealth

A family establishes an ecclesiastical trust to hold their real estate, investments, and other assets. By transferring ownership to the trust, they shield their wealth from creditors, lawsuits, and taxation while ensuring it is preserved for future generations.

Chapter 3
Understanding Private Membership Associations (PMAs)

The Power of Private Membership

A PMA allows individuals to operate outside of public jurisdiction by forming a private association. This framework is rooted in the constitutional right to freedom of association.

Key Features of PMAs

1. Private Contracts: Members agree to operate under private law, free from public regulations.

2. Autonomy: PMAs set their own rules, aligned with their shared values and mission.

3. Flexibility: PMAs can be adapted for various purposes, including education, health, and commerce.

Applications of PMAs

- **Holistic Health Practices:** A PMA allows practitioners to serve members without adhering to public health mandates.
- **Educational Co-Ops:** Parents create private homeschooling groups, free from standardized testing requirements.
- **Faith-Based Organizations:** Churches and spiritual communities operate without government interference.

Benefits of Operating a PMA

- Freedom from licensing and regulatory oversight.
- Privacy in financial and operational activities.
- The ability to foster strong, values-driven communities.

Chapter 4
Combining the Power of Trusts and PMAs

A Symbiotic Relationship

When combined, the ecclesiastical trust and PMA create a powerful system for privacy, protection, and autonomy.

   1. The Trust as a Shield: Protects assets from public jurisdiction, creditors, and taxation.
   2. The PMA as the Operational Arm: Facilitates transactions, activities, and community-building efforts.

How They Work Together

A PMA serves as the public-facing entity, managing the trust's activities while keeping operations entirely within the private domain. For example:

A health practitioner uses a PMA to serve clients, while the trust holds the clinic's assets and manages its income.

Chapter 5

Breaking Free from Federal and State Oversight

Understanding the Scope of Oversight

Federal and state governments impose taxes, licensing, and regulatory requirements on individuals and businesses operating in the public domain. These controls limit autonomy, siphon wealth, and create unnecessary barriers to financial and personal freedom.

Key areas of oversight include:

- **Income Taxes:** A significant portion of earnings is taxed, reducing disposable income and investment potential.
- **Licensing Requirements:** Many professions require costly licenses and certifications.

- **Public Reporting Obligations:** Businesses and individuals must report financial activities, exposing them to audits and legal risks.

How Ecclesiastical Trusts and PMAs Eliminate Oversight

1. Operating in the Private Domain: Both ecclesiastical trusts and PMAs operate under private law, which is distinct from public statutory law. This separation shields them from government jurisdiction.

2. Freedom from Licensing: PMAs are not required to register or obtain public licenses, allowing for unrestricted operation.

3. Tax Exemption: Ecclesiastical trusts, when properly structured, are immune to federal and state income taxes.

Overcoming Fear and Compliance by Default

Many individuals hesitate to explore these structures due to fear of audits, fines, or legal consequences. However, when properly implemented, ecclesiastical trusts and PMAs operate fully within the law, offering legal immunity from these risks.

Chapter 6
Achieving Financial Independence and Asset Protection

Why Traditional Structures Fall Short

Public systems such as corporations, LLCs, and sole proprietorships are subject to taxation, lawsuits, and government oversight. Even traditional estate planning tools, like revocable trusts, fail to provide complete protection from these vulnerabilities.

Benefits of Ecclesiastical Trusts

1. Complete Asset Protection: Assets held within an ecclesiastical trust are shielded from creditors, lawsuits, and government seizure.

2. Tax Advantages: Trust income, capital gains, and estate assets are immune from taxation when properly structured.

3. Generational Wealth Preservation: Unlike traditional inheritance methods, which are subject to estate taxes and probate, ecclesiastical trusts ensure seamless, tax-free transfers of wealth to heirs.

Practical Steps to Achieve Financial Independence

1. Identify Assets to Protect: Determine which properties, investments, and accounts should be transferred to the trust.
2. Establish the Trust: Work with a professional to draft an ecclesiastical trust agreement that aligns with your goals.
3. Maintain Separation: Ensure trust assets and operations remain separate from personal finances to preserve their immunity.

Chapter 7
Building a Values-Driven Community

How PMAs Foster Shared Values

PMAs are more than legal structures—they are vehicles for creating communities built on trust, collaboration, and shared principles.

1. Faith-Based Organizations: Religious groups use PMAs to worship, educate, and serve members without government oversight.

2. Education Networks: Parents and educators create private co-ops that prioritize tailored learning experiences.

3. Local Economies: Small businesses and farmers establish trade networks within PMAs, fostering self-reliance and local resilience.

Practical Benefits of PMAs in Community Building

- **Autonomy:** PMAs operate free from public restrictions, allowing members to prioritize their collective goals.
- **Privacy:** Member activities and finances remain confidential.
- **Mutual Support:** PMAs create networks of like-minded individuals who share resources, skills, and knowledge.

Chapter 8
Thriving in Economic Instability

Economic Vulnerabilities in Public Systems

Inflation, market crashes, and government debt create uncertainty for those relying on traditional financial systems. Key risks include:

- **Devaluation of Currency:** Inflation erodes the purchasing power of money.
- **Market Volatility:** Stocks, real estate, and other public assets are subject to unpredictable fluctuations.
- **Increased Tax Burdens:** Governments facing fiscal crises often raise taxes to compensate for deficits.

How Ecclesiastical Trusts and PMAs Provide Resilience

1. Asset Diversification: Trusts can hold inflation-resistant assets, such as gold, real estate, and commodities.

2. Self-Reliance: PMAs facilitate barter systems, local trade, and cooperative economies that reduce dependence on unstable public markets.

3. Community Collaboration: Trust-based communities pool resources, ensuring stability during economic downturns.

Chapter 9

Leveraging Life Insurance for Generational Wealth

Life Insurance as a Wealth-Building Tool

Wealthy families have used life insurance policies for generations to grow and sustain wealth. By integrating life insurance into an ecclesiastical trust, you create a perpetual cycle of financial security and growth.

How It Works

1. Policy Ownership: The trust owns life insurance policies for its members, funding premiums using trust assets or donations.

2. Tax-Free Benefits: Death benefits are paid to the trust tax-free, ensuring that proceeds remain fully available for reinvestment.

3. Cash Value Growth: Whole and universal life insurance policies build cash value over time, which can be borrowed against or reinvested.

Creating a Perpetual Wealth Cycle

1. Premium Payments as Expenses: The trust funds policies, creating a recurring legal expense while securing future benefits.

2. Guaranteed Returns: Life insurance policies provide stability and predictable payouts, even in uncertain markets.

3. Reinvestment of Proceeds: Tax-free payouts are reinvested into the trust, funding new policies or acquiring additional assets.

Real-World Example: A Multi-Generational Strategy

A family establishes an ecclesiastical trust that holds life insurance policies on every member. Over decades, the trust grows exponentially through tax-free payouts and cash value reinvestment. This strategy ensures that future generations are financially secure and able to fund educational, entrepreneurial, and charitable endeavors.

Chapter 10
Creating a Legacy of Sovereignty

Aligning Wealth with Values

An ecclesiastical trust enables families to define their legacy by aligning financial strategies with their core values.

1. Education and Development: Use trust assets to fund scholarships, training, or professional development for future generations.

2. Charitable Giving: Direct trust proceeds toward causes that reflect your family's mission and principles.

3. Long-Term Planning: Ensure that trust assets are managed responsibly, preserving wealth for generations to come.

Chapter 11

Breaking the Chains of Ignorance

Recognizing Systemic Illusions

From birth, individuals are conditioned to participate in systems that prioritize government and corporate interests. This chapter explores:

- **The Illusion of Taxes as a Necessity:** How taxation is presented as unavoidable despite private alternatives.
- **Compliance Through Fear:** How fear of audits and penalties keeps individuals from exploring sovereign solutions.

Chapter 12

Leveraging a PMA and Ecclesiastical Trust for Strategic Income Donations

One of the most powerful ways to maximize the financial benefits of a Private Membership Association (PMA) and Ecclesiastical Trust is by using them to strategically allocate a portion of your W-2 income. By donating up to half of your annual income to your ecclesiastical trust, you can achieve a significant tax deduction while still retaining access to the donated funds for trust-related expenses and mission-driven activities.

This strategy, long utilized by savvy individuals and families, allows you to align your financial contributions with your personal values, reduce your tax burden, and maintain control over how those funds are used.

The Legal Framework for Income Donations

When properly structured, an ecclesiastical trust can receive tax-deductible donations as part of its mission. These donations allow the trust to fulfill its stated purpose while providing donors with significant tax benefits.

Key Elements of the Legal Framework:

1. Tax-Deductible Contributions: Donations to the trust are deductible from your taxable income, significantly reducing your overall tax liability.
2. Mission Alignment: Funds donated to the trust must be used for its mission-driven activities, which may include educational, charitable, or community-building purposes.
3. PMA Integration: The PMA serves as the operational arm of the trust, managing activities and expenses while remaining aligned with the trust's mission.

Step-by-Step Process for Donating Income

Step 1: Establish the Ecclesiastical Trust and PMA

Ensure your ecclesiastical trust is properly structured to receive donations and is legally recognized as a private, mission-driven entity. Pair the trust with a PMA to manage daily operations and community-focused activities.

Step 2: Calculate Your Contribution

Under current U.S. tax laws, you can donate up to 60% of your adjusted gross income to eligible entities and receive a tax deduction. For maximum benefit, contribute up to half of your W-2 income to the trust annually.

Step 3: Transfer Funds to the Trust

Direct the donation to your ecclesiastical trust. This transfer should be properly documented to ensure compliance with IRS regulations. Your donation is now tax-deductible and reduces your taxable income.

Step 4: Utilize Funds for Trust Expenses

Once inside the trust, the funds can be allocated to trust-approved expenses, such as:

- Operational costs for the PMA.
- Mission-driven activities, including education, outreach, and community projects.
- Asset acquisitions that support the trust's purpose.

Step 5: Maintain Compliance

Ensure that all transactions and uses of funds align with the trust's mission statement and are documented. This protects the trust's legal standing and tax-exempt status.

How the Strategy Works in Practice

Scenario: A Dual-Income Household

John and Mary both earn $75,000 annually through W-2 employment, bringing their household income to $150,000. To reduce their tax liability and align their finances with their values, they decide to donate $75,000 (50% of their total income) to their ecclesiastical trust.

1. Tax Deduction: By donating $75,000, they reduce their taxable income to $75,000, significantly lowering their federal income tax burden.

2. Access to Funds: The $75,000 donation is now inside the trust and can be used for:
- Mission-driven projects, such as funding a PMA-run homeschool co-op.
- Operating costs for the PMA, including property maintenance, utilities, and salaries for trust-aligned employees.

3. Preservation of Control: As trustees, John and Mary maintain oversight of how funds are allocated, ensuring they align with the trust's mission while benefiting their family and community.

Benefits of This Approach

1. Substantial Tax Savings: Donating half of your income significantly lowers your taxable income, reducing your overall tax burden and keeping more of your earnings within your control.

2. Mission-Driven Use of Funds: Instead of contributing to federal programs you may not support, your funds are directed toward causes and activities that align with your personal values and spiritual goals.

3. Access to Donated Funds: Unlike donations to third-party charities, funds donated to your ecclesiastical trust remain available for trust-approved uses, such as family education, community projects, or operating expenses.

4. Privacy and Protection: The funds are now shielded within the trust, protected from lawsuits, creditors, and government claims.

Key Considerations for Implementation

1. Proper Documentation: All donations must be documented to comply with IRS rules. This includes receipts, a clear paper trail, and alignment with the trust's stated mission. This is for the member to properly receive tax deductions. Remember the trust is NOT required to report or file due to it's PRIVACY!

2. Mission Alignment: Ensure that all uses of the donated funds directly support the trust's mission to maintain its legal status and tax-exempt privileges.

3. Professional Guidance: Work with experts to ensure the trust and PMA are properly structured and compliant with applicable laws.

4. Avoid Double Dipping: Do not personally benefit from the donated funds in a way that violates the trust's purpose.

Real-World Example: Maximizing Donations for Family Education

Consider Sarah, a single mother earning $120,000 per year. She donates $60,000 to her ecclesiastical trust, reducing her taxable income to $60,000. The funds are used to support:

- A PMA-managed homeschool co-op for her children.
- Operational costs for a community learning center, including books, supplies, and technology.

By using this strategy, Sarah not only lowers her tax liability but also ensures her income supports her family's education and community values.

The Legacy of Strategic Donations

This strategy, rooted in private law and centuries of precedent, has been used by wealthy families to align their finances with their values while reducing tax burdens. By leveraging your W-2 income to fund an ecclesiastical trust, you can take control of your financial future, support meaningful causes, and build a lasting legacy of sovereignty and independence.

Let your donations reflect your values—and let your values guide your wealth.

This chapter expands on the mechanics, benefits, and practical application of using the PMA and ecclesiastical trust for strategic donations. Let me know if you'd like further elaboration or examples!

Taking the First Step Toward Freedom

The Exodus Trust provides a legal and ethical pathway to reclaim your sovereignty, enabling you to step outside the system and build a life of autonomy, privacy, and security.

Conclusion
The Journey to Sovereignty

This book is your roadmap to reclaiming your sovereignty and building a legacy of freedom. By implementing the principles of ecclesiastical trusts and PMAs, you can protect your wealth, preserve your privacy, and create opportunities for future generations.

The journey begins with a single step. Take that step today and reclaim the freedom that is your birthright.

How to take action TODAY

LiveIWS and The Intelligent Banker Private Membership Association can help you achieve this sovereign freedom. We own copyrights on these trusts and work with only the strongest rated whole life carriers in cthe Nation to deliver massive cash value vortex banking policies as well as the Ecclesiastical Non Grantor, Private, Irrevocable Trust. Our Partner in NY is a Ecclesiastical Bishop with God's authority to authorize and Grant these trusts with his official SEAL. I started LiveIWS with a MISSION and MINISTRY to free the world from the levers of control that the government corporations have inflicted upon humanity for 1000's of years.

We have a team of professionals that will strategize with you and your family and we will develop a customized plan for you to go from where your at today to where you want to be in the future! The future is yours and all you have to do is make a conscious decision to GET THE HELL OUT OF THE MATRIX! Once you do that, contact us and we look forward to working with you to establish your LEGACY! Every time we create a new Estate for a family we feel we are one family closer to breaking the chains of bondage over the world so humanity can finally enter a Golden Age and we can leave our kids and amazing world to LIVE IN when we are gone! That is the point right!

God Speed!
See you at the TOP!

Follow on IG, FB or TikTok
@RealIntelligentBanker

Made in United States
Troutdale, OR
05/20/2025

31520174R00021